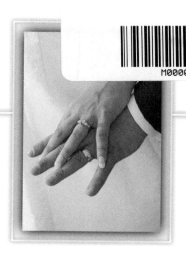

Keys to Compatibility

Opening the Door
to a Marvelous Marriage

Mac and Lynne
Hammond

KEYS TO COMPATIBILITY

ISBN 1-57399-287-9

Mac Hammond Ministries
P.O. Box 29469
Minneapolis, MN 55429
mac-hammond.org

Contents

CHAPTER 1

The Keys to Compatibility

Mac: Marriage… Is it heaven on earth?

Many single people have a utopian, idealistic view of marriage. To them, marriage is the gateway to their being loved, being happy, being fulfilled in every way. Marriage is the panacea, the ultimate cure, for their loneliness. And, yes, to them marriage holds the promise of heaven on earth!

Throughout the years in our ministry, my wife, Lynne, and I have counseled many married couples. The first time we counsel them is in their preparation to be married. That's when they're madly in love with each other and can't wait to begin their married life together. They see only wedded bliss in their future. Then sadly, the next time we counsel them (some, not all) is a year or two later when they're on the brink of divorce. What they thought was going to be heaven on earth became hell on earth.

Sadly, statistics show that about half of the marriages in America end up in divorce. This statistic, unfortunately, includes Christian marriages. Yet in spite of the statistics, most Americans still desire to be married. They just hope that their marriage will be the one that makes it. So the question is: how do we ensure that our marriage will get from "I do" to living "happily ever after?"

God's will for everyone is to live happily ever after. He hates divorce—it causes hurt and pain, not only for the husband and wife but for the children as well. God's intention for marriage is for it to be the closest thing to heaven on earth that you'll ever experience. And it is possible!

From our ministry to married couples, Lynne and I have discovered several "keys of compatibility" that will help you and your spouse achieve such unity and harmony together that your marriage will feel like a little slice of heaven! These keys to compatibility cover a variety of subjects about which the Bible has much to say. We will provide you with a beginning look at these keys, desiring to whet your appetite to learn more about and cultivate these keys in your lives.

If you're not married yet, then these keys to compatibility will become guidelines for you as you select a mate for life.

If you've just been married, then a lot of what we share will enable you to miss many of the potholes that others have fallen into.

If you've been married for 20 or 30 years, whether you think you've had a good marriage, a moderate marriage, or whatever the case may be, it can be better.

You don't have to be like that guy at his fiftieth anniversary celebration who got up and toasted his wife for *five* good years of marriage. Ouch!

The following keys of communication are general and apply to all marriages. As you read, please keep an open mind. Be willing to make an honest examination of your heart and behavior, and if you see that you've found yourself deficient in certain areas, make the determination to change in those areas.

To gain the maximum benefit from the information in this book, we suggest that couples sit down and read it together. After reading a chapter, discuss it openly and honestly. If you're both working on these keys to compatibility together, it will have a greater impact on your relationship.

By the guidance and blessing of God, you and your spouse can live happily ever after.

Let's begin!

CHAPTER 2

Exposing the Marriage Myth

Before we explore the complexities of marriage, it is important that we take a step back and expose some of the myths that many people have about marriage. Too many people walk into marriage with a starry-eyed, fairy-tale view of the journey that lies before them.

Lynne and I had an experience at the beginning of our ministry that was a point of revelation for us. It impacted us in a negative way, but from it we began to understand one of the challenges for every pastor and minister. We were counseling a very attractive, intelligent young lady who was completely devastated because she had finally realized the extent of the deception that had taken place in her life.

She said to us, "When I got married, it was like everything in my life that I ever wanted, prayed for, believed for, had come together. Everything that was worth hoping for was represented in that wedding ceremony. In one short month, I realized that I did not know the man I married."

In that one short month, she had experienced a lot of negatives up to and including physical abuse. It was another horrific example of someone's dreams being dashed. Yet over the years, this scenario had repeated itself many times. Dreams of what marriage could be become irrevocably dashed after they said "I do."

But often times these stories are not openly talked about— they are kept hidden. And even for people who hear the horror stories, they assume that it won't happen to them. Many are still in love with the idea of marriage, which is why it seems fitting to start off by exposing three myths people have about marriage.

Myth #1: Marriage = No More Loneliness

As I stated in the beginning, many people believe that marriage will solve their loneliness problem. Most single people consider loneliness a product of their being single, and as a result, marriage would be a solution to that unpleasant fact in their lives.

But Lynne and I say the same thing to every one of these people from whom we've heard this complaint: "Look, the most desperately lonely people that we have ministered to with regularity aren't single, they're married."

Loneliness is not a single's problem. In fact, it's a greater problem in marriage than it is with single people. You honestly don't know what the desperation of loneliness is until you marry expecting that relationship to solve your loneliness. That relationship has no capacity to fill the hole in your heart, and all you've done is bring another body into closer proximity to you. When that realization hits, it produces desperate loneliness. They're left without hope… "What do I do now?"

Loneliness is not solved by marriage.

The beginning of the solution to human loneliness lies in knowing where you came from. God almighty created you. When you are born again, you become a child of God. God has a plan and purpose for your life. When you begin understanding where you came from and where you're going (not only what your destiny is for this life but that you will spend eternity with the Lord), you're on the road to dealing with the loneliness problem.

Talking about the Father, Jesus said in John 8:29, "He that sent me is with me: the Father hath not left me alone; for I do always those things that please him."

Just as God tells us in Hebrews 13:5 that He will never leave us nor forsake us, Jesus also points out that He's not alone. Why?

Because He always did "those things that please Him." Jesus never felt alone because He was in perfect fellowship with God; He always obeyed His Word.

Herein lies one of the simplest truths of Christianity, yet one of the most profound. People spend a lifetime looking for God, waiting for Him to validate His reality by manifesting His presence in their lives. But the simple truth is that you will know the presence of God in your life when you begin basing your life on the direction of His Word.

When you begin basing your life on the value system of the Word—doing those things that please the Father—you'll suddenly wake up and realize that on a conscious day-to-day basis, you're walking with the Creator of this universe. You'll know God in a way you've never known Him before and you'll never experience loneliness again.

Can you see the trouble you get into when you expect your spouse to take the place of God in solving your loneliness problem? It can't happen. God alone has the ability to fill your life. Only as you conform to the image of Jesus and do those things that please God will you find yourself avoiding the loneliness problem.

Myth #2: Marriage = No More Brokenness

The second marriage myth is the belief that marriage can heal your brokenness. Many people turn to marriage out of the rejection and heartache they've experienced, or out of the emotional turmoil of not finding acceptance in society. These people haven't been able to successfully deal with these problems by themselves and they see marriage as a way to bolster up their reserves of strength, and perhaps to bring in a little pleasure to offset the pain.

Lynne: One thing that Mac and I continue to tell people is that marriage will never be a cure for your problems. That type of thinking sets you up for day after day of heartbreak. Marriage will never heal your mental or emotional calamities. There is only One that can restore your soul; His name is Jesus.

There are record numbers of young people today being brought up in homes that have been devastated by drugs, alcohol, divorce, or mistreatment. Typically, those homes aren't filled with love.

People that have experienced this loveless atmosphere are often highly motivated to latch onto another person. For example, right at the time someone feels like they are going to drown in their hurt, a five-foot-two-inch blonde life preserver floats by. That drowning person reaches out and grabs that life preserver with all that he is worth because he thinks that person will save him from drowning. This little five-foot-two-inch blonde perceives all this clutching and attentiveness as true love.

What happens next? They get married. After a few months, she blurts out, "Could you please give me a little room? I feel like you're clutching me so tightly that I can't even breathe." This pain-filled guy interprets that as another round of the rejection that he's already overwhelmed with. He feels he has lost his life preserver... he goes tilt.

I cannot tell you the number of times that we have seen this. If you are hurting or drowning in past pains, please know that marriage will never heal that pain. No matter how great you think your beautiful princess or your white knight is, there is not one person that is qualified or capable of healing your hurts.

In Luke 4:18, Jesus said, "The spirit of the Lord is upon me because he hath anointed me to preach the good news, the gospel, to the poor. He has sent me to announce release to the captives and recovery of sight to the blind. He has sent forth and delivered those who are oppressed."

Listen to how the Amplified Bible puts it: "Those who are downtrodden, bruised, crushed, broken down by calamity..." Jesus says He has come to deliver those who are in pain. He is the only one who can heal your soul. If you're single, don't look to marriage as a solution. Become a whole person in the Lord before you get married.

Myth #3: Marriage = Happiness

Mac: Thirdly, perhaps the most dangerous myth of all is the belief that marriage opens the door to happiness in your life.

Most people's unhappiness relates to their failings and shortcomings in the areas of their lives where they have felt pain and disappointment. That's why this myth is similar to expecting that your spouse can heal brokenness or somehow put balm on that pain that you feel.

The truth is marriage has no capacity to change character or personality. Yet many have that unrealistic expectation that suddenly something miraculous happens when you get married and you're not as bitter as you used to be.

If you think this way, I've got news for you. If you are a spiteful, bitter single person when you get married, you're going to be a spiteful, bitter married person. If you're a lust-filled, tormented, impatient single person when you get married, you're going to be a lust-filled, tormented, impatient married person.

As you begin learning who you are in Jesus Christ, as you begin learning what's open and available to you through Jesus, only then will your mental image of yourself begin to change. That's when you will begin to see your unhappiness turn to joy.

What is happiness? Happiness is nothing more than an emotional response to momentary external stimuli. If you'll think about it that way, how foolish is it to expect your marriage partner to stimulate all of your momentary circumstances throughout the day in such a way that you feel happy and glad.

If you're in Christ, you have something that surpasses that momentary titillation of your emotional response called happiness and it is the joy of the Lord. The Bible says that the joy of the Lord is something far deeper that transcends circumstantial stimuli. It is a product of the seed of God sown in the soil of the human heart. It's a fruit of the Spirit.

Our Sole Source of Answers

If you are looking to your potential spouse or your husband or wife to fill any of these roles—to solve a loneliness problem, to make up for the brokenness you feel, or to bring you happiness—your marriage is doomed before it starts because a marriage can do none of these things. It simply has no capacity to do that.

The answers in your life must come from only one source: Jesus.

Avoiding "Non-Compatibility"

Before we begin discussing the keys to compatibility, I'd like to say something about incompatibility. The legal profession terms the most often cited reason for divorce as "for reasons of non-compatibility." It seems to me that if we could solve the compatibility problem, maybe we'd get a handle on the divorce problem.

Webster's dictionary defines incompatibility as being incapable of association because of incongruity or disagreement or discordance.

If incompatibility is being incapable of association because of incongruity, discordance, or disagreement, then compatibility would be the ability to be in association because of the absence of incongruity, discordance, or disagreement.

If you're a Christian and you're married to a Christian, incompatibility does not apply to you. You are not incapable of a proper relationship with another Christian because according to the Bible, God made you to be a part of a larger body, the body of Christ. He's made you to be fitly joined together with other members of that body and that certainly includes your husband or your wife. That's good news for you. You're not incapable of association; you are capable of cultivating the kind of relationship that will enable you to live happily ever after.

CHAPTER 3

Key to Compatibility #1— Spirituality

No house can be built without starting off on a solid foundation. In the same way, no marriage can be built without a strong foundation. This foundation is the most fundamental area of compatibility if that relationship is going to survive. What is this key foundation?

Spiritual compatibility.

Second Corinthians 6:14 says, "Be ye not unequally yoked together with unbelievers." Period. Yes, he is talking about relationships in general. But how much more important does this admonition come to marriage—the single most intimate relationship you're going to experience in human terms?

Why can't we be unequally yoked together with unbelievers? Because you won't have fellowship. The Bible tells us that fellowship doesn't exist between righteousness and unrighteousness. There is no communion in that kind of relationship.

This does not mean in a general sense that a Christian is to have no contact with an unbeliever. Many segments of the body of Christ have taken it to that extreme. If it meant that, there would be no such thing as evangelism and the world would never be reached with the Gospel.

It does mean that there cannot be fellowship (or communion) between hearts that are saved and unsaved. Somebody who isn't saved has nothing to impart but darkness. If you marry someone who isn't saved, you are starting off your life together on the wrong foot!

This is the most essential element you must begin marriage with—you both must be believers. Otherwise, you have no common ground to begin building a life upon.

It Goes Beyond Salvation

Now the requirements of spiritual compatibility aren't met by simply marrying someone who professes to be a Christian. Spiritual compatibility entails much more than that. There are many different doctrinal persuasions within the body of Christ. There are some folks who believe God doesn't heal, and others who believe healing is for today. Some folks believe God is an angry God of judgment, and others trust He is a God full of love, mercy, and grace. Some denominations suggest the baptism of the Holy Spirit isn't of God, yet others say that's part of what we need to have in order to walk in the fullness of our Christianity.

You get the idea. There are many doctrinal persuasions in the body of Christ, and you need to be joined together with someone who agrees with you in these areas.

Yet spiritual compatibility shouldn't end with doctrinal persuasions. There are issues such as commitment to the body of Christ, participation in the body of Christ, the will of God, and financial commitment in which you and your spouse must agree on together.

Some of you may be thinking, *But, Mac, do all those things count? Are they really that important?*

The answer is a resounding yes! First Corinthians 1:10 shows us this important truth. "Now I beseech you brethren by the name of our Lord Jesus Christ that you all speak the same thing and that there be no divisions among you."

If you want to conduct your life so there's no division between you, you have to be of the same mind and the same judgment. That does not mean that you're always going to have the same opinion as your husband or wife. We're different people. We're going to have different opinions about issues that confront us. But regarding basic doctrinal issues on which spiritual compatibility is founded, there is no room for differences of opinion. On this matter, both of you must be of the same mind and the same purpose.

Paul addresses this further in Philippians 2:1; "If there be therefore any consolation in Christ, if any comfort of love, if any fellowship of the spirit, if any bowels and mercies [another translation makes that clearer; it says 'if any compassion'] fulfill you my joy that ye be like minded having the same love, being of one accord and of one mind."

Now let's apply that scripture to our marriage and tweak it to read like this: If there's going to be any consolation in Christ in your marriage, if there's going to be any comfort of love in your marriage, if there's going to be any fellowship of the spirit in your marriage, if there's going to be any compassion in your marriage, then you're going to have to be like minded, having the same love, being of one accord and of one mind.

There's no other way around it. Spiritual compatibility, the foundation for compatibility in every other area of life, comes only as you agree on the fundamental doctrines of Scripture.

"I'll Never Find Someone Like That!"

At this point, some unmarried people get a bit frustrated because these Scriptures significantly narrow their field of possibilities. You may even be thinking, *It's bad enough I have to marry a Christian, but somebody that thinks like I do on every issue? That's crazy!*

I can assure you it's much better to believe God for somebody that is like-minded with you than to jump too quickly into a relationship where somebody is not compatible with you on these crucial issues and find your life in a turmoil.

A number of years ago, I made a mistake that I will never make again. I let a couple talk me into marrying them; one was baptized in the Holy Spirit and the other wasn't. He told me that he was open and that he just needed a little more time, so I married them. Two years later, they wound up divorcing. Part of the contributing factor was the unresolved disagreement about the baptism in the Holy Spirit.

If you can't be compatible spiritually, that becomes an open door to the enemy to bring division in that relationship. I've seen this truth work time and time again. God says being spiritually compatible with your potential spouse is your most fundamental concern to avoid division in a relationship, especially in marriage.

Why Does God Care About This?

Why is this so important to God? First of all, a married couple needs to have a common plan and value system if they are ever going to walk together. Both of them need to choose a system of truth that they both agree on and adapt their lives to. As they both decide to base their lives on God's Word, that becomes a common plan that they both can endorse for their lives and a common value system that will give them guidance in the decision-making process.

Secondly, God wants you to have a common power source to deal with the storms of life. If you are of the idea that once you become a Christian, you will float along on a little puffy faith cloud and everything will be cool, you're wrong. There will be crises in life that you and your spouse need to deal with. But Jesus assured us that when the storms of life come, He is the one who has made us more than a conqueror. You can overcome the storms of life in Him. When you're married to someone who has that same power source as you, it doubles your effectiveness against the storm.

Thirdly, God says He wants us to raise our children in the nurture and admonition of the Lord so there are succeeding generations of believers to carry the plan of God in the earth. When God picked

Abraham to be His covenant partner, He knew that Abraham would command his children in the way of the Lord (Genesis 18:19).

It's vitally important to the Lord that we raise up generations of believers to follow us. If you're not spiritually compatible with your husband or your wife, your children are most likely (except by the grace of God) going to be confused and uncertain of the direction to go in life because they are getting conflicting directions from their parents.

I warn you, if you don't take the time to raise up and train your children in the Lord and instill godly values in them, somebody else will instill values in them. But they most likely won't be your values. The world is waiting, ready to saturate your kids with a belief system that is contrary to the Bible. That's why God ordained both the husband and the wife coming together to reinforce the truth of God's Word in a child's life.

Lastly, God says He wants you to be spiritually compatible because it dramatically impacts your personal relationship with God. The Bible clearly states that the marriage relationship is a type of the relationship between Christ and the Church (see Ephesians 5). Your relationship in Jesus Christ is related to the marriage relationship. If you're too selfish or proud to make the investments in your marriage necessary to make the marriage work, you'll never have a close relationship with God. The Word says that if we can't even love a man whom we can see, how are we going to love God whom we can't see? (1 John 4:20).

God's watching to see how you conduct yourself with your spouse. Will you learn the lessons that enable you to give to another person, to swallow your pride and your own self-interest in order to make the relationship work? Because if you learn those lessons in the marital arena, you'll find yourself developing a stronger relationship with God in the spiritual arena.

What if We're Not Compatible?

I'm sure there are those who are thinking to themselves, *Okay, I'd love to be spiritually compatible, but since I've married someone who is far from compatible with me, what do I do now?*

The best way to answer that is by sharing what God did for Lynne and me in our marriage. First of all, I'll give you a little background. I was saved when I was 12-years-old in a revival in a little Southern Baptist church in North Carolina; it was a very powerful experience for me.

But then my family moved a few months later to another state and we never did connect with a good church. I was young and impressionable. Having moved to a new city, I needed to make friends, and as a result, I hooked up with wrong influences. I quickly drifted away from the Lord for the next 15–20 years. I was saved, but I have to admit, you wouldn't have been able to discern it.

I was as firmly established in the world as any man could be. I liked what the world had to offer, and when Lynne got saved in 1972, it really bothered me. I wasn't happy about it because I was concerned that I may have to change a lifestyle that I had come to like quite a bit.

So we had the situation that some of you may be confronted with—one person sold out to God and the other not caring much about God at all. How do you promote spiritual compatibility in that kind of relationship so the marriage can be blessed?

Lynne followed the Lord; the Holy Spirit worked through her to change me. How? She related to me properly and in a way that wasn't offensive to me. She didn't condemn me, make me feel guilty, put me down; instead, she encouraged me, lifted me up, exalted me, and pointed me toward God. She followed the words in 1 Peter 3:1, "Likewise you wives be in subjection to your own husbands…"

This word *subjection* is referring to *submission*. It is not synonymous with obedience. Many people confuse the two terms. Submission refers to the need for godly order of authority in every human life. Every human being is required to submit to levels of authority above him or her whether it be parental authority, civil authority, spiritual authority, or authority in the workplace. According to Romans 13:1, God ordained each one of those offices of authority. We've got to relate to that authority properly. But that doesn't mean we must be blindly obedient to it. The only thing that we're required to be completely obedient to is the Word of God.

So then how do you relate properly to authority? By recognizing the need for it, not resisting it, and by realizing that the direction of the Lord will come to you through that office of authority when you have the right attitude. But before you accept direction through that office of authority, measure that direction by the Word of God. Don't ever transgress the Word of God. To the extent that you can respond to authority without being disobedient to the Word, that's what you are to do.

In the husband and wife relationship, since there is more than one person involved, there has to be somebody in authority. In this case, this job description falls to the man. Please know that this isn't a commentary on equality because we are all equal in the body of Christ.

God simply tells women to acknowledge the authority that your husband stands in. If you will do that, 1 Peter 3:1 goes on to say, "If any obey not the word, they also may without the word be won by the conversation of the wives."

Simply put, if your husband isn't obeying the Word of God, you don't have to preach to him. Lynne never preached a word to me (I'd have run the other direction!). It says that he can be won by the conversation (meaning manner of life) of the wife. This is how you change a marriage partner—you change yourself. That's what Lynne did. Because she did, I'm sold out to God today.

Lynne: Mac was always a good husband, a good father, and a good provider. We loved each other. We wanted each other's approval. He was a good lover and a good friend. So we wanted this to work.

After I became saved, I never hid my faith at home. I never stopped praying. I read the Bible like I normally read the Bible. I never gave up anything where God was concerned. But there were some things that I did do that I feel helped and maybe will help some of you.

The first thing I did was I immediately received the Bible as the Word of God and His Word to me. I never questioned that Word. I knew that God was speaking to me and so I received what He said.

Where marriage was concerned, I noticed Ephesians 5:21 said, "Be subject to one another out of reverence for Christ. Wives, be subject (be submissive and adapt yourself) to your own husbands as [a service] unto the Lord. For the husband is the head of the wife as Christ is the head of the church, Himself the Savior of [His] body" (Amplified Bible). When I read that scripture, I immediately made Mac the head of our marriage. Why? Because Jesus said he was the head. And not only did I make him the head, but I believed that he was the head, even though he wasn't acting like the head.

I released my faith that God would speak to him because God had made him the head. If God had made him the head, then I believed that God had equipped and anointed him to be in that place. Furthermore, I expected God to use him as head.

So when some type of decision needed to be made, whatever it was, I would say to him, "Well, honey, what is the Lord saying to you?"

He would say, "What do *you* think?"

I'd say, "Well, I don't know what the Lord is saying. What is the Lord saying *to you*?"

If there is one thing that my husband is not, he is not a liar. He would never say to me, "The Lord is saying to me…" if the Lord wasn't speaking to him. And the Lord surely wasn't saying anything to him at that time. But I expected God to use him. When I would say, "What is the Lord saying to you?" that put him in a position where he either had to ask God for direction or he would have to say to me nothing, and I knew he wouldn't like being in that position.

You know what that did? It oriented him toward God.

The second thing I did was that I never pointed my finger at him and said "*You* have to change." Why not? I saw in the Word of God that I needed to focus on changing me. If I became more like Jesus, then he would see Jesus in me. If he saw Jesus, then he would want Jesus.

Now let me warn you, ladies, if you think you know more than your spouse, then whether you mean to or not, you are going to project that. For me, when wives project that attitude toward their husbands, it usurps the position of authority that God has set there. The husband will sense that and he will back away from that attitude because God has set him in the place of authority. So I purposed to never do that. I never tried to change him because I knew I couldn't. I left that up to God.

Another thing is that I never saw us as separate. I always saw us together in every single thing that we ever did. So I began at a very young age in the Lord to seek God about the vision and the plan that He had for us together. I found scriptures that would cause me by the Holy Spirit to take hold of that vision that God had for us. When the vision got hazy, I would go back to the scriptures because they were my spiritual sword (Ephesians 6:17).

Lastly, I was careful about what I spoke over him and to him. I never nagged him about the things of God. When I began to walk with the Lord, the Lord began to demonstrate Himself to me. Usually when God demonstrates Himself to you, your first inclination is to go and tell everyone. But if you are married to somebody that's either an unbeliever or not walking fully committed to God, sharing those things is not wisdom.

I never spoke evil of him. When I would pray, I would pray things like, "The Lord who began a good work in you will complete it in you until the day of Jesus Christ." I'd pray, "He sits in the gates with the elders of the city," or "Lord, I thank you that you have qualified him for the call, that you have made us worthy of the vocation…"

I'll tell you, you cannot be speaking these types of things about your spouse to the Father and then go over and call Mary Jane on the phone and tell her how bad your marriage is. Your prayers won't work if you keep negating them with your words. Choose to believe and pray God's Word over your spouse. Once you've made that choice, don't hinder your prayers by speaking doubt and unbelief to others. You have to believe the Bible regardless of what others will think.

Mac: In 1 Corinthians 7, the church at Corinth had asked Paul some questions about marriage and he answered their questions in light of the law of love. In verses 12–13, he explains that if someone is married to an unbeliever, yet both are pleased to dwell with each other, they should remained married. Simply put, I was pleased to dwell with Lynne. I loved Lynne. I wanted to please her. I wanted our marriage to work.

There are some relationships where one spouse or the other is off doing his or her own thing and couldn't care less about the other one—they are not pleased to be a part of that relationship. Abuse is in evidence, whether it's physical, emotional, or some other kind. In that circumstance, the believer is not under an obligation to stay. A believing wife can't waste her life waiting on some ungodly husband to exercise his free moral agency and vice versa. I think there is a point where the Holy Spirit releases the believer and shows them that it is time to move on.

"Are you telling me it's okay for a believer to get a divorce?" you may ask.

Yes, if any type of abuse is in a marriage. Too many people have the idea that God is going to make them submit to the will of an evil person for the sake of some legalistic view of scripture. Come on! That's not the God we serve. He is a God of love.

But if two people are pleased to dwell together, like we were, then you can become spiritually compatible. Lynne never put me down. She was never a spiritual snoot, never badgered me, and never nagged me about spiritual things. Instead, she concentrated on changing herself. She knew the traits or characteristics about herself that bothered me and so she worked to change those areas. I could see changes in her. I could see her doing things to be a better wife to me and I was blown away. It had a positive impact on me and it opened me up to the things of God.

When she'd do little things like ask me what God was saying to me, it made me want to find out what God was saying to me. She did exactly what God intended for a spouse to do in this type of situation. As a result of all these things, she helped orient me toward God.

Whether you're a husband or wife, these principles apply. Praise God—He is in the restoration business and that includes your marriage. All you have to do is be willing to begin again. Lay down your pride, your self-interest, and make the decision to do it God's way. In the power of the Holy Spirit, you can become spiritually compatible and lay a strong foundation for a godly marriage.

CHAPTER 4

Key to Compatibility #2— Divine Love

Spiritual compatibility is the foundation on which your marriage must be built. After you've laid that foundation, the next thing to do is to create an environment of divine love.

My wife is the expert in our family on love. I still have a lot to learn, but I'm getting there. The fact is, if she's managed to love me for nearly 40 years in spite of some of the stuff I've done, she's got a lot to impart about the second key to compatibility—the love of God.

Lynne: When I got saved, I knew that the only way to modify my behavior was going to be through the Word of God. So I read the Bible very diligently; the first thing I learned was in First John. It said that the New Testament commandment is to believe on the name of Jesus and to love one another. Then I found another scripture that said if you would love, you would be fulfilling all the laws of God. Well, I thought, "I tell you what... this is easy. I'll just walk in love."

I quickly found out that walking in love wasn't as easy as I had thought. Seemingly every morning before ten, I would have already stepped out of my love walk. So I realized there had to be something more to this. I had a Jewish friend and she told me that there were 640 laws that the Jews had to obey. She asked me, "How many laws do you have to obey as a Christian?"

"One."

"What is it?"

I replied, "It's the law of love. We have to walk in love."

She dryly answered, "Well, I'd rather try and obey 640 laws rather than that just one."

How to Walk in Divine Love

The truth is, we *can* walk in the love of God. You may ask, "How?"

Number one: Get saved. Did you know that you can't walk in divine love if you aren't born again? Once we are born again, the love of God is placed inside our hearts (Romans 5:5). I don't know how He does it, but when you become saved, God places His love on the inside of you.

Even while understanding that truth, you may not have a clue as to how to get it out of you. You may be mean and hateful and may have just fought with your wife, but if you're a born again Christian, you can walk in the love of God. What you've got to do is learn how to get that love inside of you out.

The second thing that you're going to have to do is get 1 Corinthians 13:4–8 down inside your heart. These verses, particularly in the Amplified Bible, give you a clear definition of how God's love acts.

Remember, we are talking about God's love, not human love. Human love is the kind of love that walks all googily-eyed down the aisle, stands in front of his or her future mate, vows to love that mate forever and ever, and then later turns up in divorce court. Divine love never goes to the divorce court. Christians may end up in divorce court, but only because one or the other refuses to walk in divine love.

First Corinthians 13:4–8 begins, "Love endures long and is patient and kind…"

Human love can endure long, but it certainly isn't patient and kind in the process. Natural love always wants everybody to know what it's putting up with: "I tell you, you don't know about that man

I live with. You just don't know what I put up with," or "My wife, she nags me all day long…"

That's human love. But divine love endures long, and is patient and kind while it's enduring.

Verse four continues, "Love never is envious nor boils over with jealousy, is not boastful or vainglorious, does not display itself haughtily."

Love isn't jealous. When you're acting jealous, what is that? The flesh. "You see her? How come she got that promotion? Don't you see me, Lord? I've been waiting for my promotion for years. How come she got that promotion? I've been just as faithful."

Remember what we said earlier? The love of God is on the inside of you. You just have to reach down and let it come out by faith. You do so by speaking it with your mouth. Say to yourself, "Love endures long. Love is patient and kind. Love never is jealous." Say it over and over again. Get some three by five index cards and write on them the part you're having trouble with. Keep it with you. Confess it. And then watch the Word of God change you.

Verse five says, "It is not conceited (arrogant and inflated with pride)."

If you have pride in your life, you are in for a puncture and a great big fall (Proverbs 16:18). Divine love is never prideful.

First Corinthians 13 continues, "It is not rude (unmannerly)…" Some Christians say, "Well, I've always been rude. That's just my personality to be rude." It may be your personality, but even so, your personality needs to be overcome by the love of God. You don't have to stay rude for the love of God is not rude.

What else do we need to know about love? "…and does not act unbecomingly. Love (God's love in us) does not insist on its own rights or its own way, for it is not self-seeking."

"I have my rights." It's common to hear this during counseling sessions. It even happens to the couple who walked down the aisle, head over heels in love. One month after their wedding, they'll come in for counseling. She says, "I have my rights." He says, "Well, I have my rights." If something doesn't change, they'll be getting a divorce because of their "rights." But as Paul wrote in 1 Corinthians, divine love never wants its own rights; it always wants to bless somebody else.

A Smoke Detector and a Weenie Roaster

When I first began meditating on 1 Corinthians 13:4–8, I thought I was doing pretty good up until this point. And then I read the next part: "[Love] is not touchy or fretful or resentful; it takes no account of the evil done to it [it pays no attention to a suffered wrong]."

I picked up my Bible and went "Wait a minute, something is wrong. Lord, this can't be right. Love is not touchy? It doesn't keep a record of wrongs?" I mean, my silver-haired, wonderful Christian grandma was touchy. My momma was touchy, all my aunts were *touchies*. I came from a whole line of *touchies*. On top of that, all of them kept great records. They remembered what everybody had done to them from generations way back.

I looked at this and knew I was in trouble. Big trouble.

I'll tell you how much trouble I was in by telling you about our first anniversary. But before I do, let me warn you husbands and future husbands—never, ever give your wife anything that she *needs* as a present. Do you hear me? Never give your wife a broom. Never give your wife a mop. And never give your wife a vacuum cleaner.

We had waited for this day for so long. Mac was in pilot training, so we decided we'd take a Friday afternoon off and go up to Sea Island, Georgia. We saved up our money to go and we were so happy when the trip finally came.

When we were driving to our destination, I could see that there were two anniversary presents on the back seat for me. I had visions that those boxes contained a beautiful dress and a diamond ring. After we arrived at the hotel, I started to open my gifts. I couldn't believe it. I thought Mac was playing a joke on me because when I opened the first box, there inside was a weenie roaster.

Just so you understand what I was going through, let me tell you about weenie roasters. I hate hot dogs. Mac loved hot dogs. I about gagged whenever I had to cook a hot dog for him. The reason I hated hot dogs so badly was because someone told me when I was a little girl that wieners were made out of ground up pig's eyes. So I hated hot dogs. The other gift wasn't that much better—when I opened the other box, I found a a smoke detector inside.

There are two sides to every story, so I'll let my husband tell you why he got the weenie roaster.

Mac: I was a Second Lieutenant. You don't make a lot of money as a Second Lieutenant and so we were buying hot dogs instead of hamburgers. Lynne didn't like them so she didn't take much care about how she fixed them. She'd boil them and they'd burst and they wouldn't fit in the bun. So from my perspective, we needed a weenie roaster! And I bought the smoke detector simply because it was the latest invention that came on the market. I thought it would be a good thing to have. I was wrong. Let's just say that I've never made that mistake again. Ever!

Lynne: As I said, divine love doesn't take an account of evil done to it. Yet I wasn't walking in that part of divine love yet. Every time I had an opportunity, I would bring that up to him for five years. I would remind him of the weenie roaster and the smoke detector that he gave me as an anniversary gift. As I said before, I was in big trouble. I was one of the touchiest people you had ever seen. So I worked to change that in me by writing down on index cards "Love is not touchy. Love is not fretful or resentful. Love never takes account of an evil done to it nor does it even notice a suffered wrong."

I put the cards in strategic places of attack. For instance, I put one in my car because I was often tempted to get into the flesh there. I'll give you an example. One day, I picked up my kids from school. They hopped into the car and after a quick hello they said, "I'm starving. What's for dinner?" Isn't that always the first thing they say?

When I told them we were having meatloaf, all three of them in unison fell back into their seats with their eyes rolling back into their heads. My oldest child was the most dramatic of my kids, and he would grab his throat and start gagging, "Ahhh meatloaf. I hate meatloaf. It's like dog food." My second son, who was a little more controlled and tried to act more mature, would cross his legs, slam his schoolbooks down, and say, "I guess I just won't be eating dinner tonight. I was going to have Johnny over, but even now I won't be eating." Our youngest one—she was kind of the whiner—would say in a weepy voice, "Meatloaf... I'm so hungry and I hate meatloaf. It has oatmeal in it and onions and I hate it. Sally always gets pizza at her house..."

When my kids went on like that, I had to remember that love is not touchy, fretful, or resentful. It never notices a suffered wrong. So you can see why I put them on the dashboard in the car.

Coffee, Crackers, and a Dose of Divine Love

Now the worst place of attack was my kitchen. So I took my scriptures and put those index cards everywhere. And wouldn't you know it, the worst tester of my love was my darling husband. We are sweethearts, and I love him dearly, but he truly tested my love. That's why I put up all those little cards in my kitchen. I would say them all day, every day, over and over and over again. Over time, I began to change and the breakthrough in my behavior began to come.

I remember one night Mac came in for dinner, and my love walk was tested. I had made a big pot of soup. Now in the south, where Mac and I are from, it takes all day to make soup. I labored all day over this soup, tasting every few bites to see how it was. He came in from work, walked over to the stove, and casually said, "Hmmm, what's for dinner?"

He lifted the lid, looked in, and replied, "What's in this soup anyway?"

As I felt myself slipping out of my love walk, I remembered the scriptures. Instead of taking offense at his question, I calmly let him know what some of the ingredients were. As we sat down to the table, another attack came! While eating the soup that I had lovingly labored all day to make, he said, "You know, my mother makes awfully good soup. You should call my mother and ask her what she puts in her soup."

Mac: Can you believe I said that? I really was that stupid!

Lynne: Of course, he knows now that wasn't the most thoughtful thing to say. Thankfully, the love of God started to move in me and I acted on the Word. I said, "You know what? I should call her. That would be a good idea. Does she make some kind of soup that you like better than this? I want to be a good wife to you and bless you with soup that you like." (Before I was saved, you know what I would have said? "Let me tell you what you can do with the soup…")

There was a night in particular that sticks out to me as a time when the love of God began to bubble out of me. I had a PTA meeting at 6:30 at night. Mac came home at 5:30 in the evening. I was kind of in a rush to get ready to go to the meeting. That afternoon was the first cold snap we'd had, so I made chili. I even went so far as to make a separate pot of chili for him that had hot sauce in it, because he likes hot chili but the rest of us don't. I thought, *He will be so happy.*

I decided to make him cornbread as well. He just loved my cornbread and I knew he would be so blessed by it.

So he came in, sat down, and just as we were about to eat, he said, "Where are the crackers?"

I said, "Honey, we don't have any crackers tonight. I made you some cornbread."

He replied, "I just don't feel like cornbread tonight."

You know what? I didn't even have to get my index card out. Something started to happen inside me. The love of God started to well up on the inside of me—I kid you not—and I had this overwhelming desire to get in my car, go to the grocery store, and buy that man some crackers.

I said, "Honey, I want you to have some crackers. I'm going to the store."

"Oh no, you don't have to go to the store." He said, "I know you're going to be late for your meeting if you go to the store."

"No, I've got to get you some crackers."

As I'm walking out on my mission to get crackers, he said, "By the way, we're out of coffee, too."

I said, "Okay!"

Guess what was on special at the store? Crackers and coffee!

Do you see how you walk in love? You put the Word of God in your heart and in your mouth. You say it over and over, and believe it in your heart—it will become part of your actions.

Verses 6–8 of 1 Corinthians 13 says, "It does not rejoice at injustice and unrighteousness, but rejoices when right and truth prevail. Love bears up under anything and everything that comes, is ever ready to believe the best of every person, its hopes are fadeless under all circumstances, and it endures everything [without weakening]. Love never fails [never fades out or becomes obsolete or comes to an end]."

Mac: I serve God today because of the changes I saw in my wife. I watched her change over a year and a half or so, and I saw the difference that God made in her life. Watching her change made me hungry for what she had.

There is one other aspect of love I want to emphasize and that is the Greek word *agape*. In the Greek New Testament, we see 150–160 references to the word *love*. All of them except for 15 are the word *agape* or a derivative of it. Agape is the divine love that Lynne's been describing; it's a love that gives. It is not contingent upon what somebody else does. It is a pattern of life based on giving to other people.

The essence of a successful relationship is two people who understand the need to give. They understand the need to change a pattern of life that has formally been self-centered and begin to focus it outward to other people.

The natural mind says, "If I give to others, who is going to look after my interests?" I'll tell you who will—God. He'll transform your relationships in such a way that you won't be able to believe you didn't do this before. That's divine love—the environment you need to build in order to strengthen your compatibility with your mate.

CHAPTER 5

Key to Compatibility #3— Communication

Can two walk together, except they be agreed?
— Amos 3:3

Without agreement you will not experience compatibility with your spouse, even if you've built a foundation of spiritual compatibility and created an environment of divine love.

So the question becomes, how can you and your spouse come to a place of agreement when you both are two people with different opinions?

You come to a place of unity by becoming skilled in the third key to compatibility—the art of communication. Communication is not something that just happens because you're a human being. It is a skill that must be developed, especially if you want the kind of conflict resolution that will help bring you to compatibility in your relationship.

Communicating—It's Talking *and* Listening

Before delving into this subject, we need to get rid of the stereotypical image of the macho, strong, silent guy who doesn't do anything but grunt a few times a day. That won't cut it, guys. On the other hand, ladies, if you think you can get back at your husband by giving him the silent treatment, that isn't going to cut it either.

Communication involves more than just wanting your way. According to Webster's Dictionary, communication is the exchange of ideas or information. For communication to occur, there has to not only be someone transmitting information but also someone receiving information. If I'm flying along in my airplane and I press my transmitter and say a bunch of words into the radio, communication hasn't occurred unless there's a ground station that received my communication and responded to it. If you give your mate a piece of your mind, communication hasn't occurred, contrary to what many of us may have formally believed. Communication has to be received; it's a two-way street.

Let's add to this, God's definition of communication found in Ephesians 4:15:

> *But speaking the truth in love, may grow up into him*
> *in all things, which is the head, even Christ …*

Did you catch that? It is not enough to simply be truthful. Truth can be used to hurt; that's why truth must be spoken tempered by love.

I think everyone would consider themselves to be basically a truthful person. No one really considers themselves to be a liar, deceiver, or manipulator. Most people understand the importance of being truthful in their marriage. And yet all too often, we are found shading the truth, exaggerating stories, telling "little white lies" in our daily communication.

I'm reminded of a fellow we ministered to a long time ago. His wife wasn't present for this particular meeting. He was having marital problems and he'd come to talk about them. I discussed the subject of communication lightly with him and made mention of the fact it was important to be truthful in your communication with one another and he said, "I am. I'm a truthful person."

As the discussion went on, it came out that he was having a problem with lust and fantasizing about other women. I asked him what his wife thought about that. He said, "What? My wife doesn't know about that."

I replied, "I thought you said you were truthful with your wife?"

"Yeah, but I couldn't tell her that."

"You ought to tell her. If she knew you were having a problem with lust and fantasizing about other women, she'd help you fix it, I'll guarantee you."

It's important that we avoid defining truth based on what seems appropriate for us at that particular moment, like this man had done. There is a way to level with your spouse about any issue that is potentially divisive in that relationship. There is a way to appropriately communicate things that the enemy would like to use to magnify and produce schism in your relationship. But you have to be willing to do so and to understand the absolute necessity of telling the truth in a loving way that isn't going to hurt the other person.

Avoiding Corrupt Communication

The Lord talks more about communication in Ephesians 4:29:

> *Let no corrupt communication proceed out of your mouth. But that which is good to the use of edifying that it may minister grace unto the hearers.*

A lot of people may casually read this verse and assume that "corrupt communication" is a reference to profanity or speaking badly about somebody. But this verse goes on to define corrupt communication as anything that does not edify (build up) or minister grace unto the hearer. Any communication that doesn't cause the listener to experience the grace of God or to be built up is not godly communication. It's corrupt.

If we put together those two definitions of communication, communication can be defined as a loving impartation of the truth in a way that will encourage, edify, or build up somebody else. This doesn't mean you can't admonish or correct. If it's delivered properly, admonishment causes somebody to be built up and to grow and mature in the Lord. So we're not talking about avoiding the negatives or the things that need to be changed.

To some of you, this may not sound like a great revelation, but if you want your marriage to work, then this is something you need to take to heart and begin making a priority in your relationship with your mate.

The Purpose of Communication

The reason for becoming a skilled communicator is not so you can win your argument with your husband or wife. It isn't so you can impose your will on the other person or get your way. The primary purpose of becoming a skilled communicator is for conflict resolution.

Most married people who are having problems don't even recognize their differences as something that needs to be resolved. Very often they unconsciously assume they've got to live with all the differences and disagreements that are apparent in their relationship. But God says that you need to walk together in agreement. As a result, you have to make it a priority to resolve disagreement.

What is the most important consideration when we talk about effective communication? There are many things to consider, but I want to focus on this one in particular: your spouse is almost always going to have a different perspective regarding the issues you confront in your relationship. The greatest challenge in communicating with your spouse is coming to understand your spouse's perception—not only to understand it but to appreciate it. Most of us are so concerned with promoting our perspective that we never even make an effort to understand the other person's opinion.

Men, God gave you your wife because she has a perspective you need. Women, God gave you your husband because he has a perspective you need. When you both shift your perspectives to appreciate your spouse's view, you unleash immeasurable force in your life for good. You will improve the quality of your marriage.

Lynne: It's a matter of working together as a team. His perspective is important. My perspective is important. Yet even with teamwork, some conflicts are not resolved in five minutes of sitting at the dinner table. Some conflicts may take years to work through or for a person's perspective to be changed.

For instance, when we were first married, I was a fanatical perfectionist where my house was concerned. Mac used to joke that when he got up in the middle of the night to go to the bathroom, when he came back, his side of the bed would be made. It wasn't quite that bad, but almost. From my perspective, everything I was doing was for the purpose of keeping the house clean. But it went way beyond that. Take your shoes off, clean your drawers, straighten your sock drawers—I wasn't even aware of the bondage I was putting my household in. I about drove my family crazy.

But over the years, through communication with my family and my husband, I began to change my perception. I had to realize that my house was a place for people to come and take refuge. My house wasn't a military base where everybody conforms to a particular way of doing things. We worked together as a family and helped each other to understand.

Your Divine Safeguard

One other point I'd like to mention about communication is that agreement between the spouses is a divine safeguard in your marriage. Although Mac and I don't often have a decision we're in disagreement about, if we can't come into agreement about something, we go with his decision because he is the head of the household.

Mac: God intends it to be that way. But this is part of the trust level that is built up over years of functioning that way. If you have had a pattern of behavior in your relationship that has promoted distrust, then when it comes time to make a decision, you'll be wondering if your spouse is trying to promote his or her own agenda. If that type of thing is going on in your relationship, you need to work that out and begin to trust that you each are really looking out for the other person in your decision making.

Agreement is important because when the two of you flow in agreement and harmony, there isn't anything that will be restrained unto you (Matthew 18:19). You and your spouse make up a powerful team.

When you realize that, you'll also see that if she says no, she's not doing it to be ornery so you don't get your way. God's using her to set up a red flag for you—you had better rethink it or pray a little more about it. Even in business decisions that I made before I came into the ministry, it was important to me to have her opinion. She knew nothing about airplanes or business, but I'd go to her anyway and ask her what her thoughts were. If she had a funny feeling about it, it didn't happen. Because to me, that was a flag. I knew God had provided her input as a divine safeguard.

If you'll adopt a fresh perspective and join together in agreement in viewing the issue in that way, God can release a tremendous positive force for change in your relationship. You'll experience a great deal of blessing.

Listening Carefully, Speaking Softly, and Using Wisdom

I want to give you what I think are the three most important considerations for you in learning and understanding your spouse's perspective. Now these aren't any great revelations. Many of you know these things. But we've seen marriages fall apart all the time because people aren't acting on these truths.

James 1:19 points out the first one. "Wherefore, my beloved brethren, let every man be swift to hear, slow to speak, and slow to wrath." We usually have it reversed. We're quick to wrath, quick to speak, and we don't listen that well anyway. But, as God puts it, the best communicators are the best listeners.

By the way, listening doesn't mean token silence while you're thinking up a retort to what they're saying. It means that you hear with your heart what the other person is saying so you can gain a glimpse into why they feel the way they do and what their perspective really is.

The second consideration about communication can also be found in James 1:19. And that is, anger distorts communication. When you're saying something out of anger, a lot of times you don't even mean what you're saying. On top of that, the person on the receiving end of your anger becomes defensive. They put his or her walls up and don't hear a thing you say. Communication on both sides of the exchange becomes distorted.

Anger is a godly emotion, and there's a way that it can be expressed correctly (the Bible refers to it as righteous indignation). But when you allow your anger to be expressed incorrectly toward another person, you can rest assured, it'll distort the communication. You must be able to control your anger and communicate in a proper, godly way.

You may say at this point, "I can take care of mine, but what about my spouse's? They get angry all the time when we're trying to talk. Can I do anything about that?"

Yes.

Look at Proverbs 15:1, one of my favorite verses in the Bible. "A soft answer turneth away wrath: but grievous words stir up anger." Your response to a person is either going to stir up anger or it's going to turn it away.

Since I learned this truth, it has been really fascinating to watch the Word work. I've had people mad enough to wring my neck, and then I'll say something just as soft and as loving as I can like, "I am really sorry this happened. What can I do to make it right with you?"

It's like puncturing a balloon and all the steam goes out. I love to watch it happen; I learned it from my wife, who is a master at soft answers. Long ago before I had a handle on my flesh, I would get righteously indignant because she would do certain things I didn't like. Boy, I'd let her know I was mad, but she would look at me so sweet and say, "I'm so sorry, Honey. I didn't mean to hurt you this way." And then, I'd almost get mad because I couldn't be mad anymore. It truly does work—a soft answer diffuses anger.

Our last consideration regarding communication is wisdom. When it's time for you to say something about your perspective, there's a godly way for you to say it. James 3:17 explains what godly wisdom is:

> *But the wisdom from above is first of all pure*
> *(undefiled); then it is peace-loving, courteous*
> *(considerate, gentle). [It is willing to] yield to reason,*
> *full of compassion and good fruits; it is wholehearted*
> *and straightforward, impartial and unfeigned (free*
> *from doubts, wavering, and insincerity).* (Amplified)

Wise communication is based on the Word of God, the only source of pure and undefiled truth. When you communicate with your spouse, are you basing your thoughts on the Word of God? Is your communication peace loving and promoting unity? Are you "willing to yield to reason," even when you think you are right? Is your communication merciful, allowing your spouse to make mistakes? Is it without partiality? When you speak, do you act on what you say or is your communication lined with hypocrisy? All of these things encompass what James describes as "wisdom from above," and it is this wisdom that needs to be part of all your communication.

Ultimately, if you'll listen and properly deal with anger in your relationship, you can begin gaining insight into your partner's perspective. Then as you speak, measure your communication with godly wisdom. You will experience a breakthrough in your relationship and it'll open wonderful change to you.

Remember, communication is the only way that you will resolve conflict and walk together in agreement. Good communication centers around seeing the perspective held by your spouse, understanding it, appreciating it, and then coming to a common perspective of a higher truth. It is the only way compatibility will be true for you and you can experience the blessing of living happily ever after.

CHAPTER 6

Key to Compatibility #4— Sexual Compatibility

Sex.

It's a touchy subject that not many religious people want to talk about. Religiosity has planted the idea in some people's minds that it's inappropriate to talk about sex in a godly manner at church. And yet those same people will watch TV programs or movies that contain rather graphic descriptions about sexual encounters.

It isn't right to be silent about this important subject just because we're in a "religious" setting. We need to be able to talk openly about significant issues in our lives, especially when we discuss these issues from a godly perspective. And there are very few topics more significant to a successful marriage than sexual issues.

It's virtually impossible to talk about sex and avoid not saying anything that might be offensive to some or make others uncomfortable. In this chapter, I'm going to be direct in what I say. But my intention is not to offend or to be offensive. Please keep an open mind as you read the following.

Giving Sex a High Priority

People often assume that a good sexual relationship in a marriage flows from a good marriage. In other words, if the husband and wife are basically compatible in their relationship in other places, then the sexual relationship will be good also. On the other hand, if the sexual relationship is bad, it's a product of the marriage having broken down somewhere else.

Both of these are dangerously wrong views to hold. Why? Because it sets up sexual compatibility to be a casualty of other problems in the marriage that really don't even relate to it.

(It isn't hard to see that happening. I mean, if there's an unresolved point of conflict between a husband and a wife that generates resentment or anger, that can bleed over into the marriage bed, and potentially affect the quality of the sexual relationship.)

Usually it's kind of an unconscious thing—sex is either good or it isn't. But that's not the way God intends it to be.

The sexual relationship can be pursued and shaped in a way that it impacts your whole marriage. It is a causative effect, not simply the fruit of something that is going on.

> *Therefore shall a man leave his father and his*
> *mother and shall cleave unto his wife and they shall*
> *be one flesh.* (Genesis 2:24)

That term *one flesh* has a broad application. It is referring back to the time when God created man in one body of flesh. Remember the original creation? All of the components that made up male and female were housed in one body of flesh called Adam. Genesis 5:1–2 confirms this truth. "This is the book of the generations of Adam. In the day that God created man in the likeness of God made he him, male and female created he them and blessed them and called their name Adam in the day they were created."

Following this, God took a rib from Adam, formed Eve, and then took a portion of those personality components within Adam and made woman. Very simply, when a man comes to his wife in marriage, that's the only way either party can once again become complete—one flesh.

God said that He created man as a complete being to exercise dominion, authority over this earth and all that is in it. We like to talk about having dominion over our circumstances. We have authority over the obstacles that stand between us and the will of God. Yet that's only true for somebody operating as God created Adam— in one flesh: the completeness, harmony, agreement, and concord that was God's creative purpose for man. Once woman was taken from man, the only way that completion can ever be realized again is for a man and woman to come together in a godly marriage as one flesh.

(If you're single, please don't assume that you will be incomplete and not as useful until you get married. That's far from the truth. God hasn't left you out—He knows you're single. The Bible clearly says that God is a father to the fatherless and a husband to the widow. God is your portion in whatever stage of life you are in right now.)

Let's go back to Genesis 2:24 for a moment. Most Bible scholars agree that the terminology used here, "a man shall cleave unto his wife," has its most specific analogy to the sexual union. Sexual union is the most intimate physical experience that a person can enter into with another person as the outworking of that place of harmony and agreement.

This truth has some interesting implications. James 2:17 says that faith without corresponding action is dead. The sexual union is the natural, corresponding action to our profession of faith that we're going to walk in a place of one flesh with our husband or wife. It is that corresponding action that makes the faith you're extending to your marriage come alive.

You cannot ignore the sexual relationship. It is what makes everything else work. If you ignore it, you have limited your marriage experience to something well below what God had in mind, not only as it regards the marriage bed but everything else as well. You can't come to a place of agreement, concord, and oneness in your marriage without being right in the marriage bed.

One reason I want to begin with this emphasis is because we have met many people who have said, "We haven't had sex in years." I've also heard people say for one reason or another, "This isn't an important part of our relationship. We've come to a much deeper intimacy in the Lord. We just don't need to have sex that much anymore."

Look at what Paul wrote in 1 Corinthians 7:3–5:

> *Let the husband render unto the wife due benevolence: and likewise also the wife unto the husband. The wife hath not power* [The Greek word used means authority] *over her own body but the husband and likewise also the husband hath not power over his own body but the wife. Defraud ye not one the other, except it be with consent for a time, that ye may give yourselves to fasting and prayer; and come together again, that Satan tempt you not for your incontinency.*

God is saying it is so important that we properly address the sexual needs in our marriage that you don't even have the right to exercise that authority in sexual matters over your own body. That's the emphasis He places on it.

I do want to address something that has been an abuse of this scripture. There have been some husbands that have used this scripture in conjunction with the scripture that says the marriage bed is undefiled to bring all manner of worldly perversion into the marriage bed. Husbands will say to their wives, "You've got no power over your own body. See the Bible here? You got to do whatever I want you to do." There have been some terrible perversions brought into the marriage bed that way. That's a wrong perspective of the marriage bed. Stand back and ask, what does God want for the relationship? One flesh. That means harmony, perfect in agreement, concord. If either party to the marriage relationship is humiliated by, degraded by, or sickened by something that the other party wants to do, it shouldn't be done. One flesh symbolizes perfect agreement, concord, and harmony.

Those verses in 1 Corinthians 7 simply point out to us the premium that God puts on meeting each other's need in order to have a successful marriage. As Paul points out in the last part of verse five, if you don't treat the marriage bed with this much regard and put this high of a priority on it, Satan will tempt you.

I encourage you to root out religious thinking about the sexual relationship and place a high priority on it in your thinking. Your marriage deserves it.

Commons Hazards to Sexual Compatibility

There are some things that I have come to consider as common hazards to sexual compatibility, things that will make it difficult for the marriage bed to be fulfilling to either partner. I'm certainly not an expert on sexual behavior, but after many years of ministry, we've come to learn many things while ministering to married couples. As a result, I have been able to draw some conclusions about common problems.

I've never found people who are having problems in their marriage who have said "Oh but our sex life is great." Problems in marriage and problems in the marriage bed go hand in hand. Which comes first, the chicken or the egg? I don't know. But they always go together.

What we hear then are the things that obstruct compatibility. The first thing is very simple, so simple that it almost seems unnecessary to mention. Frankly put, you have to do the things that will make yourself sexually desirable to your spouse. I would assume you married your spouse just a little bit because you were physically attracted to them. Isn't that right? (I've never heard of anybody marrying someone that they had no attraction for physically.)

For many, the flames of passion could be rekindled by simply paying more attention to appearance. I've had some people come for counseling not knowing why their marriage has gone cold, and I'm looking at them thinking, *I think I have some insight into this,* but I can't really share it. Think about it for a moment. It's hard to want to have a major sexual encounter with hair rollers and face cream when you come home from work. I imagine it would be just as hard to have a meaningful sexual encounter with somebody that's got a big old hairy pot belly and hasn't shaved for two days or brushed his teeth.

I'm telling you the extremes in order to make a point. Within the confines of our own home, we often become too comfortable and fail to keep ourselves presentable or desirable in a fashion that would foster sexual attraction.

Instead of viewing it as extra work, view it is an expression of your love to your husband or your wife when you get up and do everything you can to make yourself look good even though nobody else will see you that day except for your spouse.

The second possible obstacle to sexual compatibility is for the ladies. One of the greatest hazards is the failure of a wife to recognize the frailty of the male ego when it comes to matters of sexual performance. There are things that God put in a man to make him the way he is. To make him sexually aggressive and very aware of his sexuality essentially has to do with the propagation of our species.

Ladies, I want to assure you that your husband needs to know without a doubt that he is the world's greatest lover. There is only one person that can reinforce that truth in his life and that is you. It's important for you to encourage him during the act of love. You can do that by simply responding to your man. If your tendency is to lay there like a "corpse" until the whole thing is over, that will feed into your husband a sense of failure. If I may be so blunt... during intimate times, there needs to be a "little wiggle" and a "little giggle." He needs to know that this is ministering to you and you're enjoying it. Reinforcing your husband's confidence in his performance will do a lot to enhance the success of the marriage bed.

The third obstacle to sexual compatibility is aimed at guys. It is a husband's failure to recognize the very real need that his wife has to feel affection from him during the act of making love. One frequent and common complaint wives have regarding the sexual relationship is this: "To him, I'm just an object. I'm a piece of property—something he can use for a sexual release." Those comments are made when the man doesn't recognize the deep, genuine need she has to feel that she's loved. She needs to know that her husband isn't just making overtures to her because he has a biological need but that he loves her and this is an act of love expressing his affection and the depth of that love as clearly as anything can. When she's convinced of that, the act of love becomes meaningful for her.

The fourth concern is for both parties. This may be one of the greatest contributors to incompatibility. It is a lack of knowledge, a failure of both the husband and the wife to recognize the physiological differences between a man and a woman regarding patterns of sexual response.

Men and women respond differently to sexual stimulation. As an example, men are very easily aroused visually. Women, for the most part, are not aroused by visual stimuli nearly as easily or as quickly as a man is. So you end up with a situation like this: a couple decides they're going to make love. He's sitting on the edge of the bed, watching her get undressed. By the time she comes to bed, he's ready to go! And then he's done, rolled off, and going to sleep before she knows what has happened!

This is a very legitimate problem we hear about all the time, which is a basic misunderstanding of the differences in our responses as human beings. Both the wife and husband need to understand each other's bodies—what is biologically stimulating to one and what is stimulating to the other.

In light of this, the need to communicate becomes paramount. Don't let it become a guessing game. Don't make it a deal where he never knows whether you do or don't enjoy what he does. Talk about it. Help illuminate to each other the differences between each of you regarding patterns of response.

Fifthly, the greatest potential hazard of all is infidelity.

There is nothing that will destroy the marriage bond any more quickly and certainly than infidelity or unfaithfulness to the marriage bed. But infidelity begins much sooner than most people think. Jesus points out in Matthew 5:27:

> *You have heard that it was said by them of old time, Thou shalt not commit adultery. But I say unto you that whosoever looketh on a woman to lust after her hath committed adultery with her already in his heart.*

According to Jesus, infidelity (disloyalty to the marriage relationship) begins in the mind. It covers a wide range of concerns that seldom are addressed as they should be in the body of Christ. Pornography, fantasizing in your mind, masturbation, any kind of artificial stimulation—anything that produces sexual gratification outside the marriage bed is infidelity. It will wreck the union that God wants you to have in your marriage.

Some people seem to think this really isn't a serious matter. But I can guarantee you, the surest way to destroy the desire you have for your spouse is to be unfaithful and disloyal to that relationship. If you toy around with fantasizing or pornography, if you pursue gratification anywhere other than the marriage bed, you will very quickly lose your desire for her or for him. You'll use that lack of desire as a reason to justify the continuance of what you're doing and most likely wind up in a literal bed of adultery. You must deal with these things. If you want God's highest and best, you can't allow these things to go ignored.

Sexual compatibility is important. Make it a priority in your marriage—not out of a selfish motivation to meet your needs, but out of a motivation to meet the need of your husband or wife. Be motivated to satisfy them and love them in this manner and God will make sure that your needs and desires are met.

Most importantly, be faithful. Be faithful to your spouse and the marriage bed. As you do these things, you will see this God-given aspect of the marriage relationship blossom into something both beneficial and beautiful in your marriage.

CHAPTER 7

Key to Compatibility #5— Finances

One of the most practical keys to compatibility involves something that everyone needs, not everyone has, but everyone wants—money.

Many marital problems couples often have involve money, whether directly or indirectly. You can probably imagine certain scenarios where this could be the case—the wife wants the husband to be motivated to make more money or the husband wants the wife to spend less.

Financial pressure on the family can cause a relationship to erupt in many places, which is why it is so important to study it in relation to compatibility.

The idea of financial planning, a.k.a. budgeting, may intimidate a lot of people, but it really doesn't need to be a big deal—you don't even have to be good at math. You just need to learn some scriptural principles about planning.

Financial Planning: A Collaborative Effort

Money defined is nothing more than a medium of exchange that represents the material realm. God has entrusted you with material resources in this life to manage on His behalf and to work with in the pursuit of His plan for your life. To the end that you properly manage those resources, you're going to experience success.

As mentioned earlier, a couple needs to have common goals and objectives in their lives. When you talk about goals in this natural realm, you can measure a large majority of them in dollars and cents. Buying a house, college education for your children, Christian schooling—all of these things have natural price tags attached. That's why both the husband and the wife must understand how to properly relate to money.

A husband and wife also need to have a common value system. This value system extends to the financial arena: Do you both tithe? Where does giving fit into your priorities? How much money do you give beyond the tithe?

Remember that compatibility in a marriage is a product of agreement or being in one accord. So the financial planning that we're going to be talking about must be a collaborative effort between both the husband and the wife. Yes, one of you probably manages the day-to-day finances of the family, and that's excellent, even necessary. But it is inappropriate for that person alone to determine the family's financial agenda. The planning process is intended to bring together both points of view and come up with a grand plan for the family that is a product of all that is in the wife's heart and all that is in the husband's heart. It is a joint collaborative effort.

Determining Your Long-Term Vision

In order to lay the kind of financial groundwork and planning that will produce the blessing of God, there are two main items that you and your spouse need to talk about.

First, you've got to agree on the long-range vision for the family. Look at Habakkuk 2:2:

And the Lord answered me, and said, Write the
vision, and make it plain upon tables, that he may run
that readeth it.

You must have a vision. Without a vision, you and your family are not going to make an effort toward financial planning that will cause the blessings of God to come. Without a vision, your finances are likely to go in the wrong direction.

Don't make the mistake of setting your vision too short, like a mere two to three months down the road. The best goal-setting process is to look as far ahead as you reasonably can (perhaps ten years ahead) where you have clarity and then work backwards. That keeps your intermediate and short-range goals and objectives on track and makes your pursuit of the end goal more efficient.

If there isn't clarity for the future, it should be discussed until it becomes clear. Most people don't have clarity for the future because they haven't taken the time to sit down and talk with their spouse about it at any depth. Which prompts the question, do you really want life to just "happen" to you? Or do you want to exercise some control over your destiny?

Be as clear about your goals as you can be. You're not too young to be looking 30 years down the road, nor are you too old to have a vision.

Do you want to retire early and travel a little bit? Do you want to write a book? Be a missionary? Go back to school and then start your own business?

Also, talk about your goals for your children. What kind of education do you want them to have? Do you want them to attend a Christian school? Do you want to help pay for their college education? You need to define as best you can the dollars-and-cents amount you need to work into the budget.

This planning helps determine what type of financial goals you need to make and what steps you need to take now in order to meet those goals then. If your long-range vision requires a lot of income that you don't have right now, you may need to set an intermediate goal of more schooling or preparing yourself vocationally for a job that's going to generate more income.

This is the first point of agreement that you and your spouse must come into. Don't let it become a tug of war where each of you fight to get your way. The best solution would be to combine both of your desires. If she envisions some kind of strange wallpaper in the bathroom, don't belittle her for it. Respect it. She may not understand why you need your umpteenth fishing rod. You need to respect one another's desires and allow the vision that you build to be a product of what is in both of your hearts.

I'd like to add one cautionary note about vision: Do not ever allow yourself to arrive at your highest goal. Once you begin drawing near to the long-range goals you had set awhile back, pray some more, talk some more, and set goals that are further out than that. Continue pressing in life as Philippians 3:13–14 tells us to.

> *Brethren, I do not count myself to have apprehended; but one thing I do, forgetting those things which are behind and reaching forward to those things which are ahead, I press toward the goal for the prize of the upward call of God in Christ Jesus.*

What Can We Do Today?

If we deal with tomorrow by setting goals and objectives, what then do we do about today? Proverbs 27:23 states, "Be thou diligent to know the state of thy flocks, and look well to thy herds."

What this scripture is telling us is to know the state of our present financial condition, to be diligent to know what resources you have coming in and what you have going out. You are to carefully manage the resources that the Lord has entrusted you with to this point in your life.

The fact of the matter is if you're not responsible in the management of what God has entrusted you with today, He'll not give you any more lest you squander it tomorrow.

Proverbs 21:20 says, "There is treasure to be desired and oil in the dwelling of the wise; but a foolish man spendeth it up." This is really a commentary on money management—the foolish man wasted his resources and the wise man turned his resources into something desirable. If you're not going to spend it up like the foolish man did, you need to know how much money is coming in and what your required expenses are before you can begin saving. The second thing that you and your spouse need to plan together is your day-to-day income and expenses.

Just as you need to plan your future together, you also need to create the family budget together. I learned that early on. One time, Lynne came to me for some money and I said, "Sorry, there isn't enough money to do that."

She replied, "Why isn't there enough money? I know how much the paycheck is; there should be plenty of money for that!"

You will prevent a lot of family squabbling if the both of you are knowledgeable about the cash-flow requirements.

Don't Spend More Than You Have

When you're budgeting, make sure what you spend doesn't exceed what you bring in. You would think I shouldn't need to mention this, but with the credit cards and charge accounts available, it makes it possible and easy to spend more than you make—but you can't let that happen.

I'd encourage you to make sure that your income exceeds your expenditures. If it doesn't, then you have one of two options available. Increase the income or reduce the expense.

At the top of the list of what you do with your income should be your tithes and offerings to the local church. If you prioritize it anywhere other than number one on your list, it'll wind up being an afterthought, and the consequence will be that God will not be involved in your finances.

Secondly, the next most important item on your budget is provision for your family's needs, which involves housing, clothing, transportation, and food. If the kind of house that you presently live in is too extravagant for your income (an indicator might be if it exceeds 35–40% of your after-tax and after-tithe income), you might want to think through the possibilities of changing that. That is, however, a judgment call for you to make. You may prefer a bigger, nicer house and less discretionary money for recreation.

Once you've made a budget, the both of you must agree to stick to that budget.

If you'll deal with these issues responsibly in the way that I've described, you will be blessed. Let's summarize: remember to talk and pray about a vision together, set your long-range goals, set intermediate goals and objectives, and lastly, be responsible to keep the budget together.

Financial planning—the management of the material resources God has placed at your disposal—works in concert with the other keys to compatibility. It's vital to share the same value system or this will not work. It's vital to have the love of God flowing between you or else it might create strife and division in your marriage. And it's vital for communication to be in place so that these financial matters are worked out between the two of you.

When all the other keys are in place, you can then plan your financial present and future, and the financial aspect of your relationship will not be a struggle or potential problem. Instead, it will become an avenue through which God can bless you abundantly!

CHAPTER 8

Key to Compatibility #6— Romance

The final key to compatibility is the key that ties everything together. It's the glue for the other elements in your marriage. What is that key?

Romance.

Some of you guys may roll your eyes when you hear that word. *Come on, Mac, I'm just not that type of guy.* Others may be thinking, *You want us to be romantic again? That stopped years ago!*

When it comes to romance, it's usually the men who are found wanting in this department. Most women, generally speaking, are more naturally inclined to be romantic. But romance is required from both spouses to tie all the other elements together.

I want you to think back to when you were dating. You had stars in your eyes, and you just wanted to be with each other whenever you could. Remember all the sweet things you did and said to each other. You were romantic with each other then. There's no reason for the romance in your marriage to disappear.

The reason romance disappears after marriage is because couples stop communicating their love to each other. Men are more inclined than women to stop communicating their love because they have difficulty speaking from their hearts. This is due usually because the man's sense of masculinity won't allow him to. He's too macho! Or if he does try to communicate, he makes the mistake of saying what he thinks his wife wants to hear but not necessarily what is in his heart.

In order for your marriage to survive and thrive, both of you must learn to communicate your love for each other. Keep romance alive!

Redefining Romance

Too many people define romance in terms of the passion they see in the fantasy realm of Hollywood. They see something that is scripted for the movie screen and then let that become the basis from which they form expectations of what they desire in their relationships. Others define romance by reading books that appear to have the definition of a true romantic relationship. Still others view romance solely in terms of physical or sexual attraction. In light of these misconceptions about romance, it becomes prudent to take another look at the true meaning of romance.

Webster's dictionary defines romance as an intense feeling of emotional attraction or attachment to a member of the opposite sex.

Romance is an emotional thing. It begins in our capacity as an emotional being to feel things for other people. The Bible says that we are a three-part being—we are a spirit, we have a soul, and we live in a body. The Word goes on to explain that our soulish man is comprised of our intellect (our mind), our decision maker (our will), and our feelings (our emotions).

Our emotions are the part of us that responds to circumstances or people—our feelings about life in general, our philosophical approach to life, the things that form our attitudes toward other people and things.

Did you know that your emotions produce your attitude? In fact, your attitude is the sum total of the positive or negative feelings you have about a certain person or condition of life. If you have a negative experience every time you encounter a certain person, you'll have bad feelings about that person. On the other hand, people who build you up, say good things to you, and encourage you will cause you to feel good about them.

Simply put, romance refers to strong, positive feelings toward another person. But why are these strong, positive feelings so important to your marriage? Your emotions are what provide the impetus behind the decisions you make.

"But, Mac, doesn't the Word say that we're not to be moved by what we see or what we feel—we're only to be moved by God's Word?"

True, but that is speaking in regard to decision making. You can't let your emotions direct your decision making. The Bible never says that feelings are bad; instead, when you cultivate the correct, emotional response or feelings, you give motivation or impetus to the decisions you make.

Think about the things that you do in your life. Your choices are based on what you feel the most strongly about. If you are passionate about your job, you are going to spend time working hard during your time at work. If you are passionate about your children, you are going to spend time with them. If you have strong feelings for your spouse, you are going to take time to make that relationship work.

Your emotions, especially the intense romantic feelings toward your husband or wife, are the sustaining force that motivates you day after day to invest the time and the effort that it's going to take to make your marriage good.

God's View of Romance

What does God say about romance? He doesn't use the term *romance* specifically, but He does talk about the idea of romance. In Genesis 2, He talks about husbands in particular and how they are to feel toward their wives.

> *Therefore shall a man leave his father and*
> *mother and shall cleave unto his wife and they*
> *shall be one flesh.* (Genesis 2:24)

The key word is *cleave*; that's the reason a man leaves his father and mother and it's what eventually causes him to be unified with his wife. I think many translations have rendered this word too mildly. We see most translations using the word *join*, but the Hebrew definition of *cleave* is much more revealing. It gets down to the issues of feelings, what motivates a man in terms of the way he feels toward his wife and the marriage relationship. The Hebrew word translated "cleave" is *dabaq* and it literally means: to cling or adhere and to catch by pursuit.

I like that. How many of you guys are chasing your wife around the house with the intent of catching her? It's good to chase her around the coffee table every now and then. It's even better to catch her! It should be part of what motivates you in your relationship. This isn't something we do by faith. It's a product of how we feel.

That Hebrew word also means: to abide fast, to cleave fast together, to follow close, to be hard after, to be joined together, to overtake, to pursue hard, to fit to. To me, that fully describes a guy that is in love, overwhelmed by his woman and not able to stay away from her. It's talking about romance—that's the only thing that can make a man act like this.

Ladies, the Bible also describes the romantic feelings you should have toward your husband. Ephesians 5:33 from the Amplified Bible says, "Let each man of you without exception love his wife as his very own self. Let the wife see that she respects and reverences her husband [that she notices him, regards him, honors him, prefers him, venerates and esteems him, praises him, loves and admires him exceedingly]."

Paul is talking about how a lady feels about her husband—the gleam in her eye every time she notices her man. He is her knight in shining armor. She's supposed to continue noticing him, venerating him, esteeming him, admiring him.

Clearly, God encourages romance.

Fanning the Flames of Romance

Your testimony can truly be, "I feel more love for her than I have ever felt before… and I felt a lot when we were first married!"

The question now simply becomes *how*?

The Bible told us "how" a long time ago. The Word tells us that we will reap what we sow. If you want love in your marriage, you have to sow seeds of love and then you'll reap a harvest of love. Psychologists are now catching up with the Bible. They've suggested that in order to keep romance alive in a marriage, it's a product of making deposits in each other's "love bank." (A Christian psychologist coined that term.)

We each have a love bank, which is our capacity to feel something about another person. You can cause somebody to love you madly or to be hostile toward you—it all depends on what you deposit into his or her love bank.

Before marriage in the courtship process, most people consistently make deposits into that love bank—good experiences and good feelings. You like being together. You tell each other how much you love one another. You compliment each other all the time. You go out together and do fun things. Every time you do, you're making a deposit in the other person's love bank. They're accumulating a high sum of positive points that increases the intensity of their emotional attraction to you.

After marriage, you begin to see some of the bad traits or flaws that your spouse has. Depending on how severe these flaws are, your attraction for your spouse is "tested." Add to that, people often start taking each other for granted and become lazy about expressing their love for each other. Because of this, you must deliberately and consciously make deposits into your spouse's love bank; otherwise, you'll start withdrawing more than you put in. Should it ever happen that you've withdrawn so much from your spouse's love bank that it reaches zero, you'll come to the place where your spouse no longer has feelings for you, and sadly, that's when the flame of romance dies. If, God forbid, you continue to make withdrawals from your spouse's love bank, creating a deficit, it will create an environment of hostility. Your spouse will be repelled by you instead of attracted to you.

This is a very simple truth—your mate's love bank can be filled or emptied depending on how you treat them.

Stay away from withdrawals—hurtful words and unresolved conflict. Purpose to not be in disagreement with your spouse about anything; purpose to discuss the point of conflict until the both of you can come to a point of agreement. If you want to keep romance alive, start thinking of ways you can make deposits into your spouse's love bank.

Lynne makes all sorts of deposits in my love bank. Consistently. For instance, one day I was preparing a message for Sunday's service and I had left my office to do something for about a half an hour. When I came back, there was a note on my desk from her that said, "I never thought it would be possible for me to love somebody as much as I love you."

That touched my heart. It was a ten-point deposit in my love bank. It made me want to run upstairs and tell her how much I loved her too.

For those of you who may think, "I don't have the feelings I used to have for my spouse," you can change that! That's the good news. It starts by you making a decision to begin making deposits into your spouse's love bank that will cause him or her to again feel emotionally attracted to you again. You must continue to fan the flames of your romance for each other.

Frogs, Egypt, and Disconnected Living

There are three things you need to be aware of that jeopardize romance in the marriage. The first one is one of the greatest potential hazards to a marriage—an uncontrolled or unhealthy pace of life.

Time can be a hard commodity to come by particularly in the kind of society we live in today. You get up early, work long or extra hours to get as much done as possible from sunup to sundown. It becomes even more complicated if both the husband and wife are working because even if they are working the same schedules, which often isn't the case, they wave goodbye to each other as they rush out the door to work in the morning. They come back in the evening, both thoroughly spent. After all that, it's difficult to relate to each other in a positive way in that condition.

Let's throw in another consideration called "children." Walk through this scenario with me for just a moment. Let's say during this period of your life, the primary wage earner happens to be the husband. He gets up early in the morning, heads off to work, waves goodbye on his way out, puts his tie on and finishes dressing as he's getting into his car. He comes back late that evening, maybe after dark, exhausted, only to be greeted by a wife and mother who ran out of energy around noon.

Then we have the time from five to eight in the evening that often looks like it came out of a B-grade horror movie somewhere. I'm talking bottles, diapers, baths, dinners, spills, messes, getting the kids in the tub, getting them out, getting on their pajamas, and putting them to bed. Then finally after the tenth glass of water has been delivered and all the toys are picked up, the husband and wife stagger toward the bedroom to get to bed. Romance is the farthest thing from their minds. Or if one is interested in romance, it's for sure the other one isn't interested at all.

So to keep romance alive in the midst of this kind of uncontrolled pace of life, you're looking at a major challenge.

I think back on that time of our lives with fear and trembling. I thank God that we got through it. I remember one time our family had been through about six to eight weeks where all three of our children had had some sort of sickness from earaches to runny noses. We had been up all night almost every night, off and on for five to six weeks. Plus, I had things going on in my business. I was trying to travel and be out of town. We had nearly reached the end of our rope until one night, a miracle happened. Everybody was in bed by eight o'clock!

Lynne: I'll finish the rest of this story. We used to have these small, screened-in cages for crickets, worms, whatever critter you wanted to put in it. Each box had a handle on it and you could carry it around, while keeping an eye on the critter inside. Sometimes our two boys would head off to a swamp near our house, catch a few frogs, and put them in the critter carrying cage. Sometimes they would play with them on the floor and see which frog would jump the farthest. But before we went to bed, we always made sure the critter cages were emptied of their contents.

One particular night, the boys had caught frogs in the afternoon and brought them in the critter cages into the house. Later when we were trying to get the kids to bed, Mac passed me with our daughter Lucy in his arms wrapped in a towel. He was going to the bedroom with her to get a diaper on after her bath and I was going the opposite way with the other two kids. He said, "Let's not forget the frogs."

Needless to say, we forgot the frogs, and the latch on one of the cages hadn't been tightened that well.

Like Mac mentioned, all the kids were in the bed at eight— literally, a miracle. We sat down on the couch together and we looked at each other... what should we do now? For six weeks we had been like ships passing in the night, living kind of disconnected.

We looked at each other. He got a gleam in his eye and I got a gleam in my eye and we ran off to the bedroom. We climbed into the bed together and embraced. As we started to kiss, the door flung open and Lucy screamed, "Ahhh! There are frogs in my room!"

You can guess what had happened. The frogs jumped out of the critter cage and began hopping around. Lucy was very frightened of the frogs, so we just put her in our bed and started on a hunt for the frogs. We quickly learned that the frogs wouldn't croak when everybody was stirring, making it impossible to locate them. We had to sit quietly and wait for them to start croaking again to determine where they were.

Soon, we had a symphony going. One would go "whirrr." Then another one croaked "burrr." We searched for those frogs about four hours. Finally we just gave up and went to bed with Lucy between us sucking her thumb. Mac said, "I feel like we're in Egypt. I'm Pharaoh and our house is being judged."

Sometimes we get in messes which can cause ourselves to become disconnected. That's when it's most important to stay committed. That's a big word in our home—commitment. You may spend two to three days where you're not connected with each other. If you're committed to each other, it's good to reassure your spouse by saying something like "I want you to know that I'm totally committed to you until we can get together and connect again."

It's so important that we cultivate romance in our marriages. Love is like fire; it has to be poked and fanned or else it goes out. We have to be very conscious of that in our lives together. Ephesians 5:15 says, "Look carefully how you walk." If you're going to walk in unity and one accord together, if you're going to have a real, vibrant zeal for one another, then you are going to have to watch how you walk every day.

Redeeming the Time

Mac: So how do you control the pace of life? Ephesians 5:15–17 in the King James version says, "See then that you walk circumspectly not as fools but as wise redeeming the time because the days are evil. Wherefore be ye not unwise but understanding what the will of the Lord is."

The word *redeem* means to recover something that is lost. In an uncontrolled pace in life, you'll lose the time that you could have invested in one another. God is saying you can redeem that time so that things don't turn out evil by understanding the will of God. The Amplified Bible reads this way:

Look carefully then how you walk! Live purposefully and worthily and accurately not as unwise and witless, but as wise (sensible, intelligent people), making the most of the time [buying up each opportunity], because the days are evil. Therefore, do not be vague and thoughtless and foolish, but understanding and firmly grasping what the will of the Lord is.

If we prioritize our time on the basis of the will of God, then we'll recover time that would otherwise be lost and our days won't turn out evil. So what is the will of the Lord regarding your schedule?

In terms of priority, the Bible places your relationship with God as number one. You need to give time to reading the Word and to prayer. The second priority is your spouse. Number three is your children. Number four is your involvement in getting the Gospel preached to all the world (your involvement in ministry). Number five is your career or your vocation.

I had one guy say to me, "I don't know how I can devote more time to my marriage. I talked to my boss about the need to adjust my schedule at work so I can spend more time at home. He said, 'I can't do that for you. I've got five divorced or single men who would gladly take your job, who can give 150%, who can work the hours that are required without having to sacrifice time at work in order to take care of their marriage.'"

In other words, if we want promotion and success, the work place seems to demand that extra time from us that could negatively impact on our marriage. But it doesn't have to be that way. If you want to redeem the time, then do it the way God says to.

Since He says your marriage has priority over everything except your relationship with the Lord, you need to take time every day with each other to make deposits in each other's love bank, time devoted to sharing and enjoying one another's presence.

This means you'll need moments of time together away from the children. Ask either set of grandparents to help with the kids occasionally. Hire a babysitter if you need to. But protect that time alone with each other. It will be one of the best investments you will ever make.

Don't Overlook the Small Things

The second potential hazard that would hinder romance is not discussing grievances that you have with one another. I'm not necessarily talking about unresolved conflict, but possibly something similar that would be a continual withdrawal on your love bank. This may be something that your partner doesn't even know they're doing.

Every couple needs to have the kind of discourse between them that encourages the kind of honesty to tell each other the truth, even about the smallest things. It was years before I learned that Lynne didn't like it when I had a toothpick in my mouth. I didn't really have a specific reason to have a toothpick in my mouth. I just kind of enjoyed chewing on it.

One day I had a toothpick in my mouth. All of a sudden, Lynne just blurted out, "Will you get that toothpick out of your mouth? I can't stand when you have toothpicks in your mouth." I was like "Whoa, where did that come from?" She had held that small irritation in for years. I never once knew that it annoyed her. As soon as I knew it displeased her, I stopped it immediately.

Even in small things like that, you need to communicate with your spouse what they are. Maybe it's the way you squeeze the toothpaste tube, or hang the toilet paper on the rack, or how you drop your clothes in the corner of the room instead of putting them in the laundry hamper. Whatever it is, have enough communication with each other to make sure these grievances are aired so they don't become a draw on your love banks.

Take Time to Have Fun Together

The third thing that is a potential hazard to romance in a relationship is not having fun together anymore. When you do something fun together, you're building positive shared experiences which makes major deposits in both love banks. When you courted, that's all you did. You couldn't wait to be together, to go out and have a good time together—maybe go to a movie, have a picnic, go waterskiing.

Often times after a couple has been married a while, they go their separate ways. The man has his fun on Friday nights out bowling with the guys or golfing with the gang on Saturday. The woman has her time with her friends during the week. The fun times together aren't shared anymore.

Your most fun times should be with your husband or your wife. Your spouse should be your best buddy. You should try to do things that you can do together and build a foundation of positive shared experiences together.

I'll caution you on one thing. Make note of the word *positive*— the experiences you share together should be positive in order to fill up your spouse's love bank. I learned this the hard way.

I wanted to start sharing my fishing experiences with my wife. I was in pilot training in Valdosta, Georgia, which is right next to the Okefenokee Swamp. Even though there are a few alligators in there, it had some great bass fishing and some good brim fishing. We had been married a couple of months at the time.

I didn't make enough money as a second lieutenant to rent a boat with an engine on it so I rented a rowboat and spent about two hours rowing us back into the swamp. We were going to fish for brim and bluegills, so I had a couple of cane poles and a bucket of worms.

I showed Lynne how to flick her line out with a cane pole and watch the bobber. I was in the front of the boat fishing, and she was in the back. Suddenly, I felt the whole boat jerking. I looked around and saw that she had thrown her line back over her head in preparation for tossing it out and her line had caught on a little bush on the edge of the swamps.

She kept jerking on her line to get it out of the bush. Unfortunately, that bush happened to be filled with hornets; they apparently did not like the interruption to their day. I kid you not, a black cloud of hornets rose up out of that bush. This was no laughing matter—in south Georgia, one hornet is as big as a 50-cent piece, coal black, and he'll knock you flat on your back.

This black cloud descended on the boat. In the meantime, Lynne froze. She sat still, not moving an inch. When she was a little girl, Lynne's father told her she could avoid getting stung by a bee by sitting completely still. She sat stone still and did not get stung one time! I on the other hand had a different outcome. I was up front, moving around swatting those hornets so much that I lost both oars and my watch. And I couldn't dive into the water to retrieve them because there was an alligator right there. Since we lost the oars, we had to paddle back with plastic plates. And I got stung so many times I was grounded for two weeks. I couldn't fly my airplane because my head was swollen so much. I said to her, "That is the last time I am ever fishing with you." And it was for 15 years!

So when I say shared experiences, I'm talking about positive experiences. Use some wisdom in what you decide to do together. We've had fun with fishing since then, but that trip was a major withdrawal from my love bank.

Have fun together. Be sure that your primary pleasure in life comes from times spent with your spouse. Cultivate interests in common, things that you can share that will build that foundation of shared experiences, which deposits immeasurable points to your love banks.

Remember the love bank principle. You have the ability to control how your husband or wife feels about you. If you want your romance to remain alive and well, if you want your spouse to have intense emotional attraction toward you, you can control that by continuing to make those deposits in his or her love bank. Spend time together, talking about differences, and resolving them so they don't become a drain.

It is possible to keep romance alive in your marriage. And if you've lost the romance, you can rekindle those flames of passion by beginning to make deposits in your spouse's love bank. Those deposits will motivate each of you to spend the time and effort that is necessary to make your marriage work.

Living Happily Ever After

There they are—the keys to compatibility. You begin with a foundation of spiritual compatibility. Next, create an environment that is filled with divine love. Strive to grow in your communication with your spouse—learning their perspective and not just striving to protect your own thoughts. Place a high priority on your natural, sexual relationship; plan out your financial future as well as your day-to-day living. Lastly, keep the romance alive in your marriage.

As you strive to grow, nourish, and protect these areas of compatibility in your life, you will open the door to God's blessing in your marriage. You and your spouse will be able to "live happily ever after."

Prayer for Salvation

God in heaven, I come to You in the name of Your Son, Jesus. I confess that I haven't lived my life for You. I believe that Jesus is the Son of God. I believe that He died on the cross and rose again from the dead so that I might have a better life now and eternal life in heaven. Jesus, come into my heart and be my Lord and Savior. From this day forward, I'll live for you to the best of my ability. In Jesus' name I pray, Amen.

About the Authors

Mac Hammond is founder and senior pastor of Living Word Christian Center, a large and growing church in Minneapolis, Minnesota.

Mac Hammond graduated from Virginia Military Institute in 1965 with a Bachelor's degree in English. Upon graduation, he entered the Air Force with a regular officer's commission and reported for pilot training at Moody Air Force Base in Georgia. He received his wings in November 1966, and subsequently served two tours of duty in Southeast Asia, accumulating 198 combat missions. He was honorably discharged in 1970 with the rank of Captain.

Between 1970 and 1980, Mac was involved in varying capacities in the general aviation industry including ownership of a successful air cargo business serving the Midwestern United States. A business merger brought the Hammonds to Minneapolis where they ultimately founded Living Word Christian Center in 1980 with twelve people in attendance. After almost 25 years, that group of twelve people has grown into an active church body of 9,000 members.

Today, Mac Hammond hosts a weekly, half-hour television broadcast called the *Winner's Way with Mac Hammond*. He has authored several internationally distributed books and is broadly acclaimed for his ability to apply the principles of the Bible to practical situations and the challenges of daily living.

He has been married nearly 40 years to his wife, Lynne, and they have three children and six grandchildren.

Lynne is an internationally known teacher and writer on the subject of prayer. She is a frequent speaker at prayer conferences and meetings around the world. Lynne also writes regular articles in the *Winner's Way* magazine and publishes a newsletter called *Prayer Notes* for people of prayer. She is the host and teacher for *A Call to Prayer*, a weekly European television broadcast and occasional guest teacher on the *Winner's Way with Mac Hammond*.

Under Lynne's leadership, the prayer ministry at Living Word has become an internationally recognized model for developing effective pray-ers in the local church. The desire of Lynne's heart is to impart the Spirit of prayer to churches and nations throughout the world.

Today some of the outreaches that spring from Living Word include Maranatha Christian Academy, a fully-accredited, pre-K through 12th grade Christian school; Maranatha College; Living Free Recovery Services, a state licensed outpatient treatment facility for chemical dependency; Club 3 Degrees, a cutting-edge Christian music club which is smoke/alcohol free; the Compassion Center, a multi-faceted outreach to inner-city residents; and CFAITH, an online cooperative missionary outreach of hundreds of national and international organizations providing faith-based content and a nonprofit family oriented ISP.

Other Books Available From

MAC HAMMOND
M I N I S T R I E S

BOOKS BY MAC HAMMOND

Angels at Your Service: Releasing the Power of Heaven's Host

Doorways to Deception: How Deception Comes, How It Destroys, and How You Can Avoid It

Heirs Together: Solving the Mystery of a Satisfying Marriage

The Last Millennium: A Revealing Look at the Remarkable Days Ahead and How You Can Live Them to the Fullest

Living Safely in a Dangerous World: Keys to Abiding in the Secret Place

Plugged In and Prospering: How to Find and Fill Your God-Ordained Place in the Local Church

Positioned for Promotion: How to Increase Your Influence and Capacity to Lead

Real Faith Never Fails: Detecting (and Correcting) Four Common Faith Mistakes

Simplifying Your Life: Divine Insights to Uncomplicated Living

The Way of the Winner: Running the Race to Victory

Water, Wind & Fire: Understanding the New Birth and the Baptism of the Holy Spirit

Water, Wind & Fire—The Next Steps: Developing Your New Relationship With God

Who God Is Not: Exploding the Myths About His Nature and His Ways

Winning the World: Becoming the Bold Soul Winner God Created You to Be

Winning In Your Finances: How to Walk God's Pathway to Prosperity

Yielded and Bold: How to Understand and Flow With the Move of God's Spirit

Other Books Available From

MAC HAMMOND
M I N I S T R I E S

BOOKS BY LYNNE HAMMOND

The Master Is Calling: Discovering the Wonders of Spirit-Led Prayer

The Spiritual Enrichment Series

> **When It's Time for a Miracle:** The Hour of Impossible Breakthroughs Is Now!
>
> **Staying Faith:** How to Stand Until the Answer Arrives
>
> **Heaven's Power for the Harvest:** Be Part of God's End-Time Spiritual Outpouring
>
> **Living in God's Presence:** Receive Joy, Peace, and Direction in the Secret Place of Prayer

Renewed in His Presence: Satisfying Your Hunger for God

When Healing Doesn't Come Easily

Secrets to Powerful Prayer: Discovering the Languages of the Heart

Dare to Be Free!

The Table of Blessing: Recipes From the Family and Friends of Living Word Christian Center

For more information or a complete catalog of teaching tapes and other materials, please write:

Mac Hammond Ministries
P.O. Box 29469
Minneapolis, MN 55429–2946

mac-hammond.org